THE CHANGING FACE OF

Botley

and North Hinksey

John Hanson

Robert Boyd
PUBLICATIONS

Published by
Robert Boyd Publications
260 Colwell Drive
Witney, Oxfordshire OX8 7LW

First published 1995

Copyright © John Hanson

ISBN 1 899536 03 5

Printed and bound in Great Britain at The Alden Press, Oxford

Contents

Front cover illustration: Seacourt Tower.

Acknowledgements

The author is most grateful to the individuals, organisations and librarians whose assistance and kindness made possible the inclusion of many photographs in this book. In particular he wishes to thank: Dr Malcolm Graham and staff at the Centre for Oxfordshire Studies, which includes the Oxfordshire Photographic Archive; Tim Blott, Editor, and staff at Oxford and County Newspapers; John McCabe and Malcolm Fearn of Hartwells; B.J.Harris, photographers, of 8, St Michael's Street, Oxford and the Vale of White Horse District Council.

To the following individuals, who lent photographs or recalled old memories, he expresses special thanks: Mr John Andrew, Mrs Peggy Bates, Mrs Cilla Brett, Mr Michael Daniels, Mrs Daphne Eustace, Miss Janet Farrow, Mr Graham Fuzzey, Mrs Doreen Hayward, Mr Arthur H. Hinkins, Mrs Jana Hitchcock, Mrs Olive Jones, Mrs MacNeill, Mr 'Tiggy' Morgan, Mr. Martin Palmer, Mr Herbert Parsons, Rev. J. Rowland, Mrs Judith Scarfe, Mr Ernest Smallridge, Mr Maurice Tubb, Mrs Monica Turner, Mr Maurice Waite and Mr William Woodward.

Where would we be without Henry Taunt in looking at past times? His work was of the highest quality and few local places were not caught by his camera. Not all of his photographs in this book are acknowledged.

Preface

My aim in this book has been to present a visual history of Botley and North Hinksey and thus set down a record of the many changes that have occured over the past 100 years. The greatest difficulty, of course, has been in deciding what should be included and what left out, though in some cases the quality of available photographs has been a deciding factor.

It is easy to sense nostalgia when looking at scenes long gone or reading recollections of past times. Much has been lost — the closeness of the small community, the readiness to entertain ourselves, the opportunity to wander over green fields, the skies filled only with birdsong. In some ways we have become alienated from the rural environment, though recently we have become more ready to safeguard what remains of our rural heritage. The loss of older forms of drudgery, with the wash-tub, say, and the scythe, the disappearance of great poverty and much ill-health (a lady remembers that as a young girl she had suspected diptheria and was taken to Abingdon by horse and cart along all the bumpy lanes), should remind us that we have also gained a great deal.

To supplement the visual record I have drawn where possible on personal memories, both from the individuals able to talk about earlier days and from the written word. One is constantly grateful to those who were ready to sit down and write about their feelings and experiences. I am particularly thankful here to the Reverend George King, who in 1960 wrote down his recollections of a Botley childhood; to Alice Harvey, who produced an account of her childhood in North Hinksey; Grace Taylor, who described the early days of Botley chapel; Geoffrey Turner; Donald Willis; Diana Swayne for her 'Story of North Hinksey'. K. Belsten's book on Botley Mill gave a history of the Hunt family.

Taunt's view of the Hinksey ridge from Oxford, in winter.

Botley and North Hinksey present an interesting area for study, with some diversity, for Botley was the more cosmopolitan community, seeking business from the passing highway and from its proximity to Oxford; North Hinksey was more isolated, more set in its rural ways. From the south-east of Seacourt Hill to the Hinksey ridge, the area was long regarded as one of rare natural beauty which offered stunning views of Oxford and afforded the city a favoured setting below its well-defined hills.

No wonder that Matthew Arnold, returning to Oxford on a visit in 1854, wrote to his wife: 'On Thursday I got up alone into one of the coombs that papa was so fond of . . . and felt the peculiar sentiment of this country and neighbourhood as deeply as ever.'

A view of Oxford from Hinksey hill.

I have tried in this pictorial record to draw attention to some of the individuals who contributed to the development of Botley and North Hinksey, either by establishing profitable industry or commerce, or by shaping local attitudes. That is right, but the twentieth century is also a pageant of the people, their everyday needs, deeds and dreams. This is their story.

I hope this book brings enjoyment to many and particular pleasure to anyone who has lived in the area and been a witness to the changes that have taken place. Perhaps it may encourage more people to use their camera or pen to make a record of today, which is tomorrow's history.

Introduction

Botley, 'Bota's clearing', was first settled in Saxon times, one of a string of settlements on the gravel deposits on the edge of the Thames floodplain. North Hinksey was another such settlement.

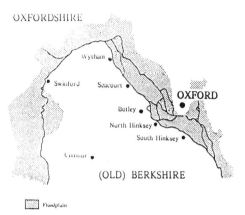

Botley was unusual because the hamlet lay across the boundaries of three parishes and manors: Cumnor, Seacourt and North Hinksey. In Medieval times Botley was relatively isolated for it had no safe direct access across the floodplain to Oxford. North Hinksey had its ferry and a causeway to Osney and the city, while Seacourt had its own river crossing and a route to Oxford's North Gate. The westward route from Oxford ran through Seacourt, over Wytham Hill to the ferry at Swinford.

Botley's importance rose as Seacourt's diminished (Seacourt was virtually deserted by 1400), and in 1524 a raised causeway was built to facilitate the journey, on foot or horseback, between Botley and Oxford in all seasons. The main westward route from the city was realigned through Botley to pick up the old way over Wytham Hill. Botley was then able to take advantage from being just outside the city boundary (the 'Shire Lacce', Seacourt Stream) and the University's jurisdiction. It became a noted drinking place. A 17th century ballad ran:

> 'Give a scholar of Oxford a pot of sixteen
> And put him to prove that an Ape hath no tail
> And sixteen times better his wit will be seen
> If you fetch him from Botley a pot of good ale'

As this early 17th century map shows, North Hinksey was then known as Laurence Hinksey, after the patron saint of the church, to distinguish it from its neighbour. It was also called Ferry Hinksey.

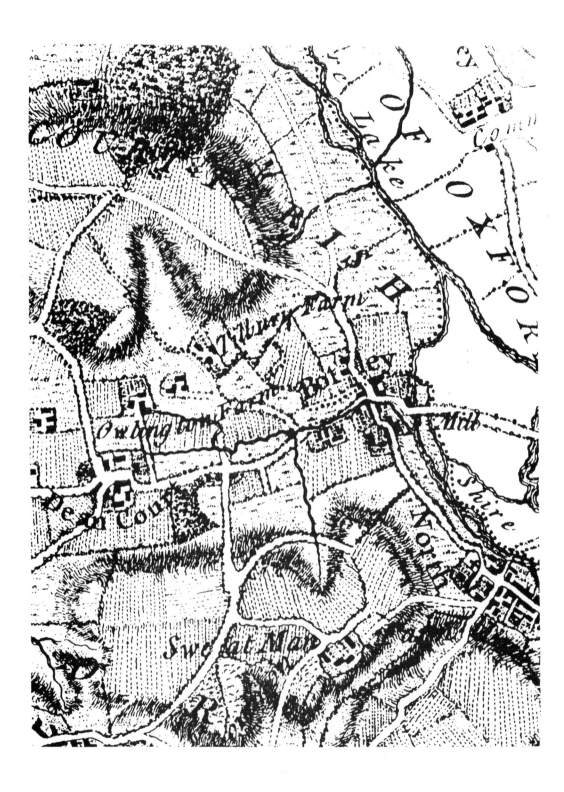

Rocque's map of 1760 is interesting. It shows clearly the old packhorse route from Botley over Wytham Hill which was turnpiked soon afterwards.

Much of the old turnpike over Wytham Hill is still evident.

The map also shows the deviation of the causeway south of the 'George' alehouse, using a narrow bridge by Botley Mill. Farmers using waggons to convey their produce to Oxford had to unload at a gate across the causeway entrance in Botley and transfer their goods to their horses until the main causeway was improved, again soon after Rocque drew his map. Swinford Bridge was built as part of the improvement of Oxford's road to the west.

A drawing, after O'Neill, shows a narrow bridge still spanning the millstream by Botley Mill in 1890.

Rocque showed Elms Farm, to the west of Old Botley. The old way to Cumnor can be seen turning south at Botley Pound.

Further road realignments occured in the early 19th century. In 1810 the Earl of Abingdon (Lord of Cumnor, Wytham and Seacourt manors) promoted a new road from Botley to Swinford along the valley (now Eynsham Road), thus denying travellers easy access to his woods and an overview of his manor house at Wytham. The road from Botley to Cumnor was turnpiked on a more direct route in the 1770s, then moved onto its present line in the 1820s.

Botley became more important to the region's developing road system but it did not grow significantly in size. Nor did North Hinksey. The lords of the manors held on to their lands. It was not until this century, the main subject of this book, that Botley and North Hinksey were overtaken by Oxford's suburban growth. Land, that gave little profit in a period of agricultural recession, was sold by the impoverished owners and exploited for residential and commercial development. Economically the area became part of Oxford; by-passes, essential to traffic flows in the wider region, intruded further upon its character. Today Botley and North Hinksey present an interesting amalgam of the old and the new, which this book seeks to illustrate.

Opposite: The centre of Old Botley.

Botley Road

The Botley road from Oxford became an increasingly important route, both for long-distance travellers and local people.

At the beginning of this century the western end of the road still ran above green meadows, liable to flooding.

Known in earlier times as Seven Bridges Road, its deteriorating conditions by 1910 led people to call it the 'Via Dolorosa'. Not the least of its miseries was the narrow hump-backed bridge by the 'George'.

In 1923 the old narrow bridge was demolished and a new one built on the main roadline. These photographs shows the work in progress.

The 'George'

The 'George' still stands beside the first branch of the Seacourt Stream as you come from Oxford, over the old county boundary. The 'George' alehouse was first recorded in 1726 when it was valued at £3 a year.. It belonged to Cumnor manor, and therefore for several centuries to the Earls of Abingdon, though it always lay in North Hinksey parish. In 1842 the 'George' boasted a stable, skittle alley and garden. The landlord was Joseph Green.

Taunt's photograph of the 'George' in 1892 shows the crowd accompanying the beating of the city bounds enjoying refreshment there. As the wall advertised, the landlord then was Fred Daniels.

Fred Daniels came from Tetsworth and settled briefly in Wolvercote and Wytham, where he plied his craft as a wheelwright. He married a Wytham girl and by 1889 had moved to the 'George', where he brought up his large family.

Fred Daniels and his son Fred are on the riverside terrace. On the right is one of the haywagons he built. In those days a landlord needed an additional source of income.

In 1920 Fred Daniels bought the nearby mill from the Earl of Abingdon and moved there. Fred Cocks became the landlord.

'The George' in 1991, when Henry Skelcher was landlord. The photograph was taken shortly before it was overshadowed by the large office block on the adjoining commercial site.

Botley Mill

A mill at Botley was first mentioned in the early 13th century. It lay in North Hinksey parish but was part of Cumnor manor, owned in medieval times by Abingdon Abbey and from the late 17th century by the Earls of Abingdon. It was partly destroyed in the Civil War but restored, whereas a mill at Hinksey did not survive.

Lord Abingdon's rent book shows that by 1795 the mill lease had been purchased by Edward Hunt. His son John, who later took over the mill, was born the following year. John Hunt died in 1886, aged 90. The family ran a corn milling and bakery business.

John Hunt 1795-1886

TYPEWRITERS,
DUPLICATORS,
FILING SYSTEMS
AND SUPPLIES.

WILLIAM HUNT

Printer and Stationer,

THE PIONEER OXFORD TYPEWRITER
DEPOT and COPYING OFFICE,

18 BROAD ST., OXFORD

(Opposite Balliol College).

Patentee of the 'Ideal' Loose-Leaf Books.

Telegrams: 'Typewriter, Oxford.'   Telephone: 917.

One of John's grandsons, Charles, who married Grace Gee, was running the mill at the end of the century. But another grandson, William (1867-1954) was apprenticed in the printing trade and worked in London and Yorkshire before returning to Oxford to establish a stationery and typewriter shop in Broad Street. Later he joined with Broadhurst to build a printing and stationery works on the Botley Road, in what became known as 'New Botley'.

This fine photograph by Henry Taunt may show Charles Hunt and family, at Botley Mill at the end of the last century. The miller employed a baker when one of the family was not avaliable for the task. He also employed a millwright until the old machinery was abandoned. In 1881 the millwrights were John Curtis from Wiltshire and his son William. In the 1890s John Curtis turned his mind to the making and repair of agricultural machinery and established his own business.

For some years until 1910, Daniel King worked the mill. He lived in a cottage next to the 'Carpenters Arms'. His son George recalled: 'My father worked the little mill on the Seacourt Stream . . . This was a one-man show; my father ground the corn, set the dough, baked the bread and delivered it by horse van round the local villages.'

Later, the Earl of Abingdon sold the mill to Fred Daniels. By then the milling was done by machines, on contract for an Oxford cornfactor. In 1924 however the mill was in such bad condition and affected by the nearby bridge building that it was demolished.

The demolition of Botley Mill in 1924.

Fred Daniels built a new house (no longer standing) nearby and the younger Fred Daniels' family grew up here. They remember the winter skaters on the mill pool with fairy lights around, the swimming in the stream, and the fishermen laying out their catch on the floor of the 'George'.

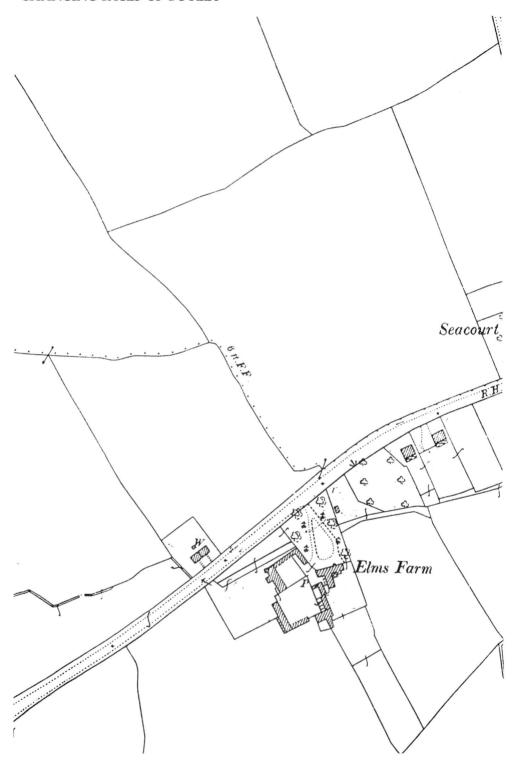

This map shows the extent of Old Botley in 1898, when the hamlet retained much of its rural character. The site of the present Seacourt Arms was occupied by two cottages - the tenants, Clack and Belcher, worked at Elms Farm across the road.

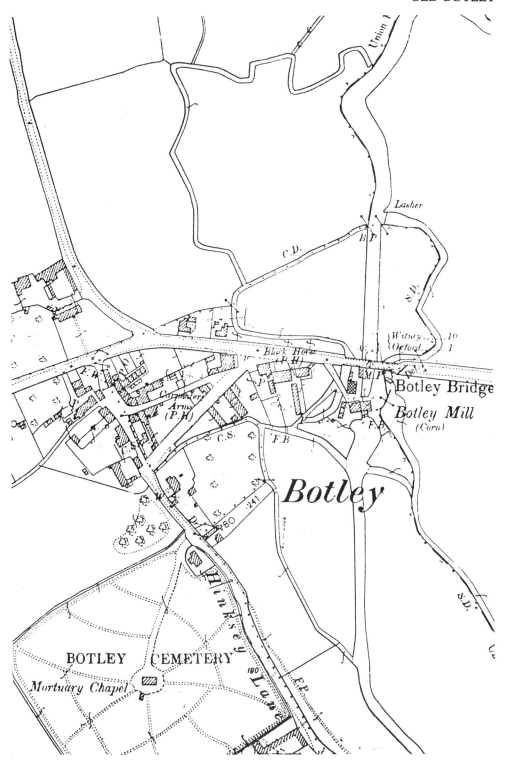

A line of dots from fields north of Elms Farm, along the main road and down Hinksey Lane, marked the boundary of Cumnor Parish then. The 'George', not named on this map, has been cross-hatched. ('P' indicated a pump, 'W' a well.)

Charles Hayman's house

This house stood close to the 'George' and in the early years of this century was owned by Charles Hayman. It is no longer standing. Its large rose garden was tended by James Bryant.

Hayman, seen here with his sister Mrs Miller, had a fishmonger's business in Oxford, getting his ice from an ice house in Hythe Bridge Street. The younger Fred Daniels worked for him for a time as a delivery driver.

Hayman had a carriage pulled by two horses. It is said he enjoyed a good standard of living.

West Way

The approach into Botley has changed considerably over this century, as these photographs show.

'It was,' George King recalled of the years up to 1920,' the age of horses'. The above photograph shows wedding guests stepping into a cab on the Botley Road in 1909.

Going into Old Botley c.1920. The motorcyclist, with sidecar, is believed to be Ralph Read. The large white building was 'North Lodge', built about 1860 for Joseph Arnstin, a solicitor. At the turn of the century it was the home of Ernest Piggott, an Oxford dealer and pork butcher. During the Second World War it was empty and used by the local Home Guard. The site is now the end on the 'Carpenters Arms' car park. On the left the 'Black Horse' public house can be seen.

Seacourt Farm is just visible beyond the turn to Wytham. On the right stood two brick cottages, Seacourt Villa and Victoria Cottage, occupied at this time by William Curtis and Joseph Read.

The view in September 1962, when a building was demolished to enable road-widening and an improvement to the Wytham turn. Oxford and County Newspapers.

West Way in 1991

The 'Black Horse'

The 'Black Horse', a public house built in the early Victorian period, was run in the Twenties and Thirties by Spencer Hancox and his wife. Their son was a motor mechanic and in 1925 they obtained a licence to instal a hand driven petrol pump on the roadside. In 1930 Halls Brewery made a successful application for a water supply to be laid onto the premises. Mrs Hancox had a reputation for 'knowing her mind' and 'told you when you'd had enough'.

The first horse-drawn buses from the city had their terminus at the 'Black Horse', as the photograph indicates.

The 'Black Horse' amid one of the floods (winter and summer) that were a regular occurence in Botley early in this century. The landlord at that time was Mrs Hartwell.

A Wytham farmer bought a horse for his wife to take a cart to market. He bought it from a butcher who had habitually stopped at the 'Black Horse'. When his wife returned from market, the horse always stopped at the door, to her great embarrassment. A typical country tale!

The day before demolition in 1991

In 1963 the licence was withdrawn and the premises were taken over for commercial use. In 1991 the building was demolished for commercial development on Minns' commercial site to the rear. 'Ah', sighed the demolition worker, 'I had many a pint in there. They pulled the beer with those old-fashioned handles'.

Buses

Travelling between Botley and Oxford, until after the Great War, meant you either walked, got on your bike, drove a horse and carriage, or used the horse-drawn omnibus service. For some years the latter service ran to the 'Black Horse', where the omnibus turned round. Later the route was extended to the foot of Cumnor Hill. William Woodward, who lived as a young boy in a cottage opposite Tilbury Lane at Botley Pound, recalled 'sitting at the apex of Eynsham Road and Cumnor Hill to watch the lovely black horses, pulling the trams, turn round to return to Oxford, having dropped their passengers'. The year was 1912. The first buses came into operation around 1914.

One of the Oxford Tramway Company's horse-drawn omnibuses.

This early bus, seen at Swinford toll bridge in 1917, served Eynsham Road on its route to Witney.

A country bus (single-decker to get under the station bridge in Oxford) of the 1920s that passed through Botley.

This aerial photograph taken in 1918 shows Old Botley expanding along West Way, with Elms Road and Poplar Road already built. But Seacourt and Elms farms remained, with their orchards, and arable land still touched the main road.

From the 1880s the name Old Botley was used to distinguish it from the New Botley. the developments within the city boundary on and off the Botley Road. By 1918 development on the Oxford side had not reached the Seacourt Stream boundary.

The line of the 1770s turnpike to Cumnor is visible across the fields running south-west from the lower road built in Botley to link it to the causeway.

The Old Centre of Botley

'A Bit of Old Botley' c.1925, looking down Hinksey Lane. The shop, run by Mrs Bull, was in the corner cottage to the left. Its boards adver-tised 'Colman's Mustard' and 'Sunlight Soap'. Mrs Bull's second husband William probably worked on the railway. For much of the 19th century it was the home of the village blacksmith. Around 1930 the cottages on the right were occupied by Trinder, Austin, Hardy and Church.

A fuller view of the cottage on the right. James Bryant is standing in front. c.1930. With the cottage beyond, it was occupied in 1660 by Thomas Wright, a farmer and alehouse keeper. The alehouse, 'The Crown', was the further building of the two.

Looking down Hinksey Lane in 1991.

This cottage in Hinksey Lane is dated '1633'. It was rented then by Joseph Cantwell. In 1647 his widow was ejected on account of 'her unchaste behaviour'. For several centuries it was a market garden. The Field family held it through the Victorian period. It was for a time semi-detached. In the 1930s it was, according to report, the home of Percy Bennett, who suffered a leg injury in the Great War, used to run a coffee stall at the bus terminus at the bottom of Cumnor Hill and who became caretaker of the new Botley School in 1938.

A view from Hinksey Lane c.1910, looking north towards Seacourt Farm in the background. The wooden building, a blacksmith's workshop in the previous century, was now a mission chapel. In 1914 it was taken over by Mrs Kitchen for a laundry.

The cottage on the left, on the corner of the main road, was in the grounds of Shaw's (later Surman's) bakery.

A closer view. The homes on the left were in Cumnor parish; those on the right in North Hinksey.

This side street, Old Botley, was formerly the main roadway leading onto Botley causeway. There was a gate across a few yards in. In 1760 a blacksmith's stood on the left corner.

The tall house at the back was built c.1770. In 1841 it was occupied by George Haynes, a man of independent means, and his sister. In the 1920s it was the home of Henry Read. The cottage to the right of it was in 1842 the home of Charles Horn, a sawyer who worked in the nearby timber yard. It was later occupied by Daniel Pimm, an agricultural labourer.

The cottages on the left were part of the property owned for centuries by the Trustees of the Poor Charity of St.Ebbe's parish in Oxford.

This brick cottage was built early in the 19th century. By 1861 it was occupied as a police house by Nimrod Elphick, a 'county policeman', who was born in Sussex. It remained a police house until earlier in this century.

These cottages, part of a terrace of six built, were probably built of Chawley bricks and tiles. They were erected in 1900 by Sydney Shaw at the end of his garden. He was a baker and builder. The buildings are typical of the period. The first tenants were Emmanuel Prickett, George Hawtin, James Bryant, Fred Moss, Lewis Kitchen and James Ridge.

This prominent house on the lane between Botley and North Hinksey was for centuries a farmhouse. In 1560 it was held of the Lord of Cumnor Manor (Sir John Williams) by Thomas Speene, a graduate of St. John's College. He also held the mill. The present house may indeed have been built by Speene. By 1891 much of the land had been taken into Sweatman's Farm and the house was home to three labouring families. Many young people will remember it for the riding stables of Miss Halliday.

Carpenters Arms

One of the first references to the Carpenters Arms by name was in a survey dated 1842, when John Parker owned 'The Carpenters Arms public house, wheelwright's shop, store room, stable, yard and garden', together with a timber yard with sawing houses

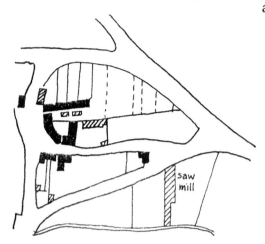

across the road on what is now an office block site. The census of the previous year had described John Parker as a timber merchant, aged 35. It is not hard to see how the public house got its name. Its earlier history is uncertain.

This section from a 150 year old map shows that the original entrance to the 'Carpenters Arms' was from the Old Botley lane. It was separated from the main road by a line of cottages and gardens. A few people still remember them.

The Oxford Journal reported in July 1899 an event suggesting that the Carpenters Arms had a loyal following:

'BOTLEY
The outing from the Carpenter's Arms, Old Botley, on Saturday proved successful. Leaving Botley at 1.30, the party journeyed to Buckland in a 4-horse brake. On arriving at Buckland a substantial dinner, supplied by Host Charles of the Lamb Inn, was partaken of. The Queen's health was drunk and the party visited the church. The rest of the evening was spent in songs, and home was safely reached after an enjoyable afternoon.'

The premises were, like much of Old Botley, vulnerable to flooding, the last serious flood occuring in 1955 when Ellis Wren was landlord.

This photograph was taken in 1978, when Frank Morris departed after 15 years as landlord. The premises have recently been remodelled to include a Beefeater Steak House but the old name has been retained. Oxford & County Newspapers.

Botley Cemetery

The lay-out of Botley cemetery with its radial paths is easily recognised on both the 1898 map and the 1918 aerial photograph (p. 26). The land here was sold by the Earl of Abingdon to Oxford city for this purpose. The lodge, in Hinksey Lane, was built in 1892 on the site of an old cottage occupied for many years by the Gardiner family.

The cemetery is of special interest in that it contains a large section for Commonwealth War Graves. A visit there provides a moving reminder of the men and women from many countries who fell while fighting for the Allied cause in two world wars.

Kelly's Directory for 1932 listed just 140 private residents (householders) in 'Old Botley', including Botley Pound. Many of the residents were in Poplar Road or Elms Road - but no houses yet south of Elms Farm. The building boom had not yet begun. The list for North Hinksey comprised only a dozen names.

Old Botley.

PRIVATE RESIDENTS.

Allsworth Noah, Botley pound
Ashfield Frederick. 28 Poplar road
Austin Mrs. W. Old Botley
Ayres David Henry, 3 Elms road
Barney Rt. Botley pound
Barson Albt. R. Old Botley
Barson Benj. Old Botley
Barson Jsph. Old Botley
Bateman Mrs. 2 New cotts
Bawdon Isaac, Wavendon cott. Poplar rd
Bayliss Thos., Alandale, Botley pound
Bennett George, 4 Elms road
Bennett George Oliver, 3 Old Botley
Bennett Jas., Glenavon, Botley pound
Bennett William Henry, 5 Old Botley
Blackwell George Henry Bertie, Rosery, Botley pound
Bradfield Frederick James, 8 Poplar road
Breakspear William, 23 Poplar road
Brentnall Edwd. H. Elms rd
Brown Mrs., Lulworth
Bryant James, 4 New cottages
Burden Fredk. Crosswell, Hinksey la
Buswell Stuart, Brookhampton, Hinksey la
Capel Alfred, Holcombe villa
Carter Garnet, 5 Poplar road
Charlton Mrs. Alfred John, Harmsworth
Charlton Reginald John, Willowdene
Cheshire Thos. Kilburnie, Botley pound
Clack Geo. A. Elms cott. Old Botley
Coates William Charles, 2 Elms road
Collins Fredk , Elmsdale, Poplar rd
Cooper James, 17 Poplar road
Cooper Lionel Jn. 24 Poplar rd
Cooper Mrs. Eaglodene
Cotton Thos. Harry, Basiltone
Cox Frederick, 16 Poplar road
Curtis Frank Rt. Brookside, Hinksey la
Curtis John T. Broad Clyst house
Curtis Miss E. M. North lodge
Curtis William, Seacourt villa
Daniels Fredk. (rear of The George r.h)
Douglas Sholto, Manor ho. Hinksey la
Durham Jsph. Briardene, Old Botley
Durham Michl. The Bungalow
Enoch Mrs. 7 Elms rd
Enoch William John, 1 Poplar road
Field Edwd. Jn. Nalders
Field Hubert, Gothic ho. Old Botley
Finch Mrs. 11 Poplar road
Fletcher Mrs. Sunnyside, Botley pound
Floyd Mrs. Botley pound
Gatchfield John W. Bexhill, Botley pound
Goddard Thos., Elm lodge
Green Geo. Old Botley
Hall Ezra, Crossness, Botley pound
Hamilton Walt. Roselare, Elms rd
Hardy Arth. Thos. Old Botley
Harris Alfred, 30 Poplar road
Harris Frank, 4 Poplar road
Hastings Mrs. 15 Poplar road
Hathaway Arth. Willow cott
Hawtin George, 12 Poplar road
Hayman Chas. Old Botley

Herbert James Philip, Athlone
Herbert Wltr. Jn., Hill view, Botley pound
Hill Chas. Harry, Overdene, Botley pound
Hill George, Mayfield, Botley pound
Hill Jn. Tadmus Orme, Botley pound
Horne Geo., The Shrubbery, Botley pound
Howe Arthur Swithin, Oak dene, Botley pound
Hudson Alfred, Pernes cot. Hinksey lane
Hudson Henry, 1 Hinksey lane
Jarvis Frederick Ernest, 6 Poplar road
Johnstone Hy. R., The White ho. Elms rd
Kimber Arth. Firle Leigh
King Danl. Old Botley
King Miss Maude. Old Botley
Kitchen Mrs. Bessie Florence, 4 Old Botley
Lane Geo. Old Botley
Launchbury James, 2 Poplar road
Lovegrove Wilfrid, Kenilworth
Morbey Charles, 18 Poplar road
Morris Henry John, 1 Elms road
Moss Frederick William, 3 New cottages
Moyle Mrs. 36 Poplar rd
Mullington Albt. E. Caerwen, Botley pound
Neale Alfred Leonard, 13 Poplar road
New Edward James, Hursley. Elms road
Norridge Edwd., Glengary. Botley pound
Norton Wilfred Jn. 22 Poplar rd
Parker Mrs. Sarah, Old Botley
Parker Wltr., Arcadia, Hinksey la
Pearce Albert Victor, 9 Poplar road
Pearce Mrs. 21 Poplar rd
Penny Frank, The Gables, Poplar rd
Pickett Mrs. 6 New cottages
Pimm Mrs. 10 Poplar road
Pratley Harry, Ferndale
Qurtish Mrs. Eliz
Read Alfred, 5 New cottages
Read Harry, South view
Read Joseph Barnes, Victoria cottage
Richards George, 26 Poplar road
Ridge Chas. Botley pound
Ridge James, 1 New cottages
Robinette John Walter, Tramore
Saunders James, 8 Elms road
Sawley Danl. Hinksey la
Shelton William, Singletree, Botley pound
Shorter James, 2 Hinksey lane
Sims Jsph., Penville, Poplar rd
Smith Chas. Armand, Restenneth, Botley pound
Smith John, Home Lea
Stayte William, 7 Poplar road
Steptoe Wm. Rosewin, Hinksey la
Stevens Arnold, 3 Poplar road
Sturch Henry Richard Fowler, Hopewell
Sweetzer Wltr. Highelere
Thomas Percy, 5 Elms road
Thornett Geo. Hy. Sea court
Tilby Ivan, Henley cott. Elms rd
Timms Wm., Lilliers, Hinksey la
Trinder Arthur, Ivyhurst
Trinder Mrs. L. Old Botley
Tuck Arth. Geo., Granta, Botley pound
Turner Albt. 19 Poplar rd
Turner Thomas Arnatt, Tanglewood
Tyler Chas., Sea Court ho

Walker Harold, White bungalow, Poplar rd
Warburton Mrs. S. The Limes, Botley
  pound
Webb Mrs. 14 Poplar road
Wheeler Wm. The Cottage, Old Botley
Woodbridge Frederick Geo. 20 Poplar rd
Woodward Miss R., Marcott, Botley pound
    COMMERCIAL.
Bennett Percy Geo. refreshmnt. rms
Botley Women's Institute
Bull Emily (Mrs.), shopkpr
Carey Ernest Geo. grocer, & post office
Cocks Fredk. Chas. The George P.H
Cooper Jas. carrier
Curtis John & Sons, haulage contractors &
  mechanical engineers, Botley works.
  Phone, Oxford 2420.

Curtis Stephen Hy. dairyman, Thatched
  cott. Hinksey la
Grove Thomas William, cabinet maker &
  joiner, 6 Elms road.   Phone, Oxford 3766
Hancox Spencer, The Black Horse P.H
Hancox Spencer, jun. motor engineer
Harper Harold, keeper Botley Cemetery,
  Hinksey la
Hinkens & Frewin, bldrs. (yard)
Howse Stephen E. dairyman, Elms farm
Surman William, baker
Titcombe Ernest Albt. police constable
Wilson Albt. insur. agt. Eastfield, Elms rd
Wren Ellis F. The Carpenters' Arms P.H

Joseph Barnes Read was born in Botley in 1866, when his father was living in the cottage at the top corner of Hinksey Lane. Joseph married Rachel Hedges; he worked for some years delivering bread for the nearby bakery. The directory for 1932 showed him to be living at Victoria Cottage, on the north side of the main road.

Some Botley Personalities

This photograph of families gathered together a hundred years ago is a reminder of how religious faith was a binding force in the community.

In the 1920s and early 30s, Old Botley was still a quiet place. There was only one street lamp. Many of your needs were supplied by local people, though you had little choice. Your bread came from Mr Surman's bakery — he'd bake your cake if you took him the ingredients. The Elms Farm dairy supplied your milk. Fred Moss repaired your shoes. Bill Bennett delivered your coal. Mrs Bull ran the local shop. People did not feel part of Oxford, though youngsters looked to it for entertainment. 'I remember going to the cinema with my father for the first time, to see Laurel and Hardy, at the 'Majestic' on the Botley Road'. The 'Majestic' was the one- time ice-rink, now the site of M.F.I.

'There is nothing, absolutely noth-ing, half as much worth doing as simply messing about in boats'. Two of Fred Daniels' boys, and probably two Austin brothers, among those en-joying an outing on the river in the 1930s.

Botley Football Club in the 1919/20 season. The team played on Botley Meadow across the river, close to the site of the present Park and Ride. Known names, left to right: standing — Alfy Hastings, — —, — —, Reg Read, — —, Arthur Curtis, (capped figure behind was George Shepherd from Farmoor, a keen supporter), Archie Read, 'Son' Kitchen, Gilbert Read; sitting — 'Titchy' Hardy, — —, — —, Ernie Read, Sid Farrow (a son of Mrs Bull by her first marriage, he married Helen Curtis; became a Post Office inspector), — —.

1909. Guests at Seacourt Farm for the wedding of Albert Turner and Constance Hartwell. The bride, born in Osney, was the daughter of widow Sarah Hartwell, who ran the 'Black Horse' across the road. On the left: Beatrice Turner, Albert's sister-in-law, and her daughter Phyllis.

Four young Botley men on their motorcycles in the 1920s. From left to right: Ernest Read, Alfred Read, Spencer Hancox jnr., and Reg Read.

The Women's Institute 'en tableau' in the 1930s. Back row: Nellie Farrow (née Curtis), —
—, Edith Curtis, Mrs Eliza Herbert, Mrs Bryant, Mrs Wheeler, — —, Mrs Smith; front
row: — —, — —, Rose Witham.

The W.I. first met in a building close to Elms Farm but in 1933 Lord Harcourt
agreed to sell a plot in Hinksey Lane, where the present building was erected.

Celebrations on the coronation
of George VI, as the procession
nears the top of Hinksey Lane.
The sailor (Bill Church) and
soldier (John Read) stand
beside Brittania (Doreen
Smith). The lady on the right
was probably Mrs Enoch.

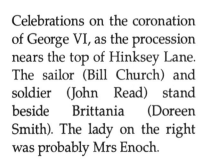

Botley Chapel

Baptist worship began in Botley in 1882 when James Launchbury started to hold services in his cottage. His son, also an agricultural labourer, was a tenant at Seacourt Farm in 1891.

In 1894 St Ebbe's Parish Charity Trustees leased to George Parker of Botley 'cottages and a building formerly a blacksmith's shop, now used as a chapel'. This was the separate wooden building, known to the congregation as 'Workman's Hall'. Four years earlier the Abingdon Herald had reported: 'Special Services were held in Mission room on Sunday, and at 6pm the building was crowded before the time specified'. A public meeting in 1892 agreed 'to hereby unite to form a Christian Society of Protestant Dissenters from the Church of England, usually assembling for Divine Worship in the Workmans' Hall, Old Botley'.

The Botley members became members of the 'mother church' in New Road, Oxford. In summer, meetings were also held in a field (now under the A34) to which was brought a wagon where speakers addressed the congregation, 'sometimes at considerable length'. In 1912 thoughts were directed towards a new building, though local funds amounted only to £2. 19s 1½d. Funds were however found to purchase a site, in what is now West Way, from Lord Abingdon for £35 and a new chapel was opened on 6th November 1913.

The chapel, with 'New cottages' beyond, in July 1976.

Grace Taylor, a grand-daughter of James Launchberry, later recalled: 'I am told that we three girls were taken to Chapel in our long baby clothes ... I remember a story that was often told how one of us commenced to cry during the sermon and the preacher stopped and said 'Let us sing a chorus till the little one has settled down'.

Sunday school trips were 'a trip up the Eynsham Road in a Hay wagon being driven by Jim Nixey or Old George ... We arrived at Dean Court, the home of Mr and Mrs Nixey, and trudged our way up to the Mount, now I believe very close to the new Cumnor by-pass, to play races and swing on the swing already put on one of the big trees. Then the women brought up the tea in big washing baskets; sandwiches, cakes and, of course, those lovely sticky lardy cakes made by Mr Surman the baker next door to the Chapel'.

'Is there anyone', Grace wondered,' who can remember Mr Bryant, who often took the offering, marching down the aisle in time to any Voluntary being played?' Quite a few, actually.

During the war the schoolroom was used to help evacuees. In 1953 it was decided to acquire a more central site on the old Southern By-Pass, now Westminster Way. Enthusiasm was high during the ministry of Richard Hamper.

Left to right. Back: Emmanuel Enoch, Brian Jones, Mr Blatchford, David Thomas, Percy Telling. Front: Rev Richard Hamper, Mr Alder, Dr Gordon Francis.

In 1968 the last service was held in the West Way chapel. The building was later adapted for commercial use.

The Rev. John Matthews and John Hitchcock. 1968.

A commemorative tablet for the new Baptish Church being laid by Emmanuel Enoch, a Deacon.

The new Baptist Church. The tablet is being moved during renovation work in 1995.

The Rev. John Matthews, Baptist minister in 1968.

Farming

In the last century most people in Botley worked on the local farms. Even within living memory, farming was important. 'There were wheatfields then from Botley to North Hinksey', recalled a former resident. The meadows near the river provided good pasture for dairy cattle. One farmer was very obstinate and when, in 1916, the clocks were put back to give daylight saving, he insisted on keeping to 'God's time' – and missed the milk trains to London.

Harvesting at Seacourt Farm c.1920. The worker may have been Ted Surman. This field was near Botley Lodge and the path up to Wytham Woods. Elm trees were prominent in the landscape then. Albert Turner ran the farm.

Elderly residents remember sheep being grazed in the field by Poplar Road on Tuesday evenings in readiness for being taken into Oxford market early the next morning. Until 1935 a pair of cottages stood on the corner of Poplar Road. The occupants, Clack and Belcher, worked at Elms Farm. In 1935 the Seacourt Bridge Inn was built on the site.

Jack Webb, who lived as a boy at Tilbury Farm, helped his father look after the many horses kept there. His father had been a drover and Jack himself would earn a shilling by driving cattle, bought at Newbury market, from Oxford station along the lanes to local farms. He remembered the steam ploughing and the machinery hired out by Curtis's in Botley.

One of the local farms was Elms Farm. It can be traced back as a property to medieval times. John at the Nutbeam paid tax in Botley in 1327 and in 1540 a large farm called Nutbeams ('Nut Trees') was rented from the lord of Cumnor manor by William Buckner.

The Elms Farm house, which many people can remember.

View of the farm from road c.1935.

The Development of Elms Farm

The freehold of Elms Farm, like that of other Cumnor properties, was sold in the 1920s by Lord Abingdon and his creditors. It was acquired by Stephen Howse, who came from Yarnton. Elms Farm dairy supplied local homes and parts of Oxford; some milk no doubt went onto the London milk train. Mrs Willis, who lived in Hythe Bridge Street in the early years of the century, had milk from 'Howes of Elms Farm'. It was delivered at 5 am, when she was preparing breakfast, and was put into a jug she left overnight on the doorstep.

In 1935 Howse was given planning permission to erect a parade of shops on the main road. Berkshire planners, anxious by that time to reduce ribbon development, required that the shops be set back from the road. Elms Parade opened in 1937, its architecture in the popular Art Deco style. The first shop to open was Wissett's the chemist, where the Post Office is now. The Botley post office then was still over the road at Carey's on the corner of Poplar Road. Above: the area in 1937.

Elms Parade, shown here in 1961, was a significant development for it brought to Botley a sense of suburban identity and the wider range of retail outlets which the rapidly growing local community, including Cumnor Hill, demanded. Photo: Oxford & County Newspapers.

Nearly thirty years ago the Parade was expanded by the addition of a precinct at the rear and the last vestiges of the old farm were gone. The precinct, which was later improved with covered walkways, opened with a range of shops which included Bishop's store (now Budgeon's), Pottle's the chemist, Carter's hardware shop; Barclays moved into larger premises from the front. This picture was taken in 1990.

Elms Parade in 1991.

NORTH HINKSEY DIRECTORY.

Green Mrs. M. A. New Haven, Elms Farm estate

Greenop Geo. Sandwith, Southern By-pass rd

Greenwood Jas. Edwd., Robreen, Elms Farm estate

Grundy Alfd. Rd. 74 Southern slope

Hainge Arth. Ivydene, Botley rd

Halliday Cecil A. Manor ho. Hinksey la

Hamblin Chas. Hy. The Rookery, Elms Farm estate

Hamilton Wltr. Rosslare, Elms rd

Hammond Wm. Rd. Wyndham, Elms Farm estate

Hancox Spencer, Clovelly, Cumnor hill

Hans Mrs. 56 Southern slope

Hardy Arth. Thos. Old Botley

Hardy Eric Aug., Gypsy Hurst, Hurst Rise rd

Harries Jn. Harding, Fairfield, Southern By-pass rd

Harris Alfred, 30 Poplar road

Harris Frank, 4 Poplar road

Harris Harold, 23 Poplar rd

Harvey Cecil G. Homeleigh, Poplar rd

Harvey Joe, Highfield, Southern By-pass rd

Hastings Mrs. 15 Poplar road

Hathaway Wm. Willow cott. Botley pound

Hawkins Hy. T. Knowle cott. Hinksey la

Hawtin George, 12 Poplar road

Hawtin Jesse Wm., Dalkeith, Southern By-pass rd

Hayman Chas. Old Botley

Hayter Mrs., Cranborne, Cumnor hill

Hayward Wm. Hy. 62 Southern slope

Herbert Hubert, Upweys, Hurst Rise rd

Herbert James Philip, Athlone, Botley rd

Hewitt Alec J. Stanway, Elms Rise estate

Hickmott Wm. Geo. 33 Southern slope

Hicks Mrs., Birchover, Southern By-pass rd

Hill Arth. Dudley, Uplyme, Southern By-pass rd

Hill Christphr. Chas. 48 Southern slope

Hill George, Mayfield, Botley pound

Hill Geo. R. Westland, Elms Farm estate

Hill Wm., Bagendon, Botley pound

Himms Fredk. Hubert, Cornerways, Elms Farm estate

Hope Jsph. Tintern, Elms Rise estate

Horsman Ernest, Wood Lea, Hurst Rise rd

Howe Arth. S. Oak Dene, Botley pound

Howland Arth. Geo. 9 The Crescent, Elms Farm estate

Hudson Alfred, Pernes cot. Hinksey lane

Hudson Ernest, Elms Farm estate

Hudson Henry, 1 Hinksey lane

Hurst Claude, Polruan, Southern By-pass rd

Ingram Thos., Cartreiv, Elms Farm estate

Inness Geo. Wm., Amroth, Botley pound

Inness Harry, Elmhurst, Elms Rise estate

Isaacs Mrs. Wyndham, Hurst Rise rd

James Fredk., Liebling, Elms Farm estate

James Geo., Cosheston, Southern By-pass rd

Jarvis Frederick Ernest, 6 Poplar road

Johns Howard M. 6 Hinksey la

Johnson Wm. Goodwin, 6 The Crescent, Elms Farm estate

Johnstone Hy. R., The White ho. Elms rd

Jones Wm. North Lea, Hurst Rise rd

Kilbee Reginld. Abel, 2 The Crescent, Elms Farm estate

Kimber Arth. Firle Leigh, Botley pound

King Albt. Chas., Michaelton, Southern By-pass rd

King Arth. Ernest, 7 Southern slope

King Geo. 7 Poplar rd

King Miss Maude, Old Botley

Kirby Edwin R., Sydea, Southern By-pass rd

Kitchen Mrs. Bessie Florence, 4 Old Botley

Lambert Jn. Wm. 52 Southern slope

Lambert Mrs. L. M. Little Beechwood, Hurst Rise rd

Lanchbury Jas. 2 Poplar rd

Langford Cyril Ernest, Mardale, Elms Rise estate

Launchbury Keith W., Westfield, Southern By-pass rd

Lee Mrs., Caerwen, Botley pound

Lester Arth. 3 Southern slope

Lewis Alex., St. Helens, Elms Garth estate

Lewis Wm. 10 The Crescent, Elms Farm estate

Lightfoot Newton, 12 Southern slope

Lloyd Wesley, Westholme, Southern By-pass rd

Lockwood Leonard Pearson, Elmstead, Southern By-pass rd

Longshaw Geo. Hy. 54 Southern slope

Lovegrove Wilfrid, Kenilworth, Botley rd

Lowe Mrs. St. Mary's, Elms Rise estate

McPherson Bertram Grant, Airlie, Southern By-pass rd

Marriot Gerald, Gerane, Elms Farm estate

Marsh Cecil Jn., Elmside, Hurst Rise rd

Marson Kenneth, Sunnymeade, Elms Farm estate

Mason Frank, Seacourt ho

This page from Kelly's Directory for 1937, by kind permission of Kelly's Doirectories Ltd., provides evidence of the new housing developments which in turn had created demand for more shops. Farm land did not yield good profits in a period of agricultural recession and its chief asset lay in potential development.

Arthray Road was one of the first developments in the open land then lying between Botley and North Hinksey. The houses, designed in the attractive art deco style of the period, were built in the early 1930s. Oxfordshire Photographic Archive.

Some houses in Arthray Road still retain their original features. Mrs Phillips moved into her house a year after it was built. 'There was an open field behind. We got our milk from Elms Farm and there was a dairy shop. The Parade wasn't there then'.

Some More Personalities

It's May 1968 and three local figures meet to discuss a proposal to build old people's bungalows in a field behind West Way, extending Seacourt Road. Left to right: William Palmer, chairman of Abingdon Rural District Council; Rev. J.W. Stratton, Vicar of North Hinksey; Rev. J.F. Matthews, Baptist Minister of North Hinksey.

William Tell Palmer, a wine merchant, opened the second Parade shop in 1937, in premises now occupied by the flower shop. His son has documents which show steady growth, but on one day, four weeks after opening, he took nothing and entered 'blank'. Liquor was then on quota. During the war he served in the Ministry of Labour. In 1956 he moved to the shop's present premises at 47 West Way, where his son Martin now conducts the business.

'Eighty years of rural business ended with champagne for Abingdon Rural District Council in March, 1974', said the papers. The photograph shows William Palmer of Botley, as chairman of the council, signing the last minutes. Under local government reorganisation the council ceased to exist. North Hinksey parish was drawn into an enlarged Oxfordshire, with services being the responsibility of the new Vale of White Horse District Council.

Botley Football Club: the 1958 team. Harold Cambrey, who had a butcher's shop in Elms Parade, was President of Botley Football Club in the late 1950s. The photograph shows him with the evidently successful team of the 1957/58 season. Known names, left to right, are: Front row: John Rowland, Jack Slater, Tom Evans, Basil Wheeler, Mr Cambrey, Mick Painter, 'Tiggy' Morgan (junior team coach), Ted Morgan, Jimmy Rae. Second row: 'Sudgie' Harris, Ted Smart, Ginger Rivers, Mick Barley, Eric Norris, Johnny Ward, Chris Allen, Mick Pinfold, Barrie Bridges, Ron Evans. Third row: David Rand, − −, Donald Savin, Mervyn Thomas, 'Darkey Harvey', Trevor Woodington, Mike Charlotte, Johnny Burke, Bill Wheeler. Fourth row: − Bargus, Fred Ball. Back row: Sid Farrow, − −, Danny Darcy, − Barley, Horace Evans, Ernie Smallridge (who spent many happy years teaching at Botley School).

Hubert Curtis, born 'near Swetman's Farm' in 1903, the son of John Curtis, was a local representative on Abingdon Rural District Council for twenty-five years. He served in many capacities, including Chairman; it was a period, he said, when 'politics didn't come into it'.

Hubert's grandfather had founded Botley Works and, having studied engineering at Oxford and spent several years in Australia, he joined the family business. His great hobby was flying. He joined the University gliding club after watching gliders over Cumnor Meadow in 1935. Kronstedt, an Austrian, who later died in an experimental aircraft, was the instructor. Hubert Curtis bought his first plane from Kronstedt for £80. 'It was a 'drone' or 'pusher' with the engine and propeller behind the pilot. It wasn't very fast — about 80 mph. You'll be all right, Kronstedt told me — just don't tip the wings too much'. He was given a petrol allowance for it in the war to use it as a spotter plane for the Home Guard. He eventually crash-landed it on Cumnor Hill. He enjoyed an adventurous time in the Home Guard. After the war he bought a two-seater Auster. Hubert Curtis retired to Cutts End farmhouse in Cumnor, where he died in 1993.

Raymond ffennell (born Schumacher) was a German who allegedly made a fortune in the South African diamond industry before retiring to England with his wife and daughter. He was a tenant of Lord Abingdon in Wytham House during the First World War and in 1920 bought the Wytham Estate from the impoverished Lord. He thus acquired most of the land north of the Eynsham road. An unexpired lease prevented him moving into Wytham House immediately, so a chalet was built in Wytham Woods, using some of the stone from demolition work by the 'George' for the lower walls. The family tended to spend their winters abroad, often on their ocean-going yacht. Ffennell nevertheless took a keen interest in local affairs; his portrait shows him in the pose of an English country squire. He was a generous benefactor and was anxious to save his 'sacred hills' from future building development, unless it were for an extension of the university.

Ffennell was, for a short time, in charge of the Botley Home Guard during the war.

He had a genuine interest in children's welfare and made provision at Hill End for the outdoor education of city children. His kindness to many local children is remembered. His only child, and heiress, Hazel died young and ffennell bequeathed Wytham and its woods to Oxford University.

SECTION TEN

Seacourt

The old manor of Seacourt lay between Botley and Wytham and was the site of a village deserted in medieval times. In the 16th century it became part of the Wytham estate.

This photograph from the 1930s shows the site of the deserted village of Seacourt and the former Wytham Road from Botley, now under the Western By-Pass.

Seacourt Farm began as a small estate in Seacourt manor and in 1444 was gifted by one William Fynderne, for the good of his soul, to Lincoln College. Over the centuries many of the leaseholders employed a 'farmer' as under-tenant to occupy and run the farm. Thus in 1783 the lease was held by John Foulkes, Doctor of Physic of Oxford University but the farmer was William Dover. It was then generally known as Housecourt Farm.

A view of Seacourt Farm c.1910.

'Seacourt Farm was acquired . . . by my grandfather and was farmed by his third son Bert Turner', Geoffrey Turner wrote in 1963. 'At its peak the holding comprised land on both sides of the Botley Road, including the site of the Co-operative Bakery, the field at the corner of Binsey Lane (where I saw my first circus) and other fields nearer Binsey'.

Albert Turner and his wife, seen above at the house of their neighbour Charles Hayman.

Albert and Constance Turner relaxing at the farm c.1925.

The farm was later taken over by Stephen Howse and his son Eddie. They modifed the front elevation by inserting a second front door and enlarging the windows.

Farm buildings.

In 1963 five and a half acres of land, including the farm buildings, were acquired by the Hartwell Group and developed as a commercial site between West Way and the planned Western By- Pass. 'It is a little sad', reflected Geoffrey Turner, to think that there will never again be rabbit-skins drying in the wash house or eggs to be found in the mangers or behind the ricks'.

According to the 'Oxford Times' on 20 September 1963, the farm was to remain on the site. 'It is to be embodied in the plans for a motel on that corner of the six acre site. This was one of the conditions imposed by the planners'!

Development of Seacourt Farm

Hartwells, the company which built Seacourt Tower, has a long and interesting history in the motor trade.

Alfred Hartwell began trading in Chipping Norton before the First World War and after it he established garages in Oxford: the Austin agency in Park End Street and a Ford agency in Banbury Road. During the Second World War a workshop was set up in Ferry Hinksey Road to build mobile canteens to serve workers and victims of the Blitz.

After the war the company was reorganised and diversified. Alfred Hartwell retired from the Board in 1952.

c.1953

A new site was purchased on the Botley Road, now West Way, opposite Seacourt, and the Ford commercial vehicle business was moved there in 1954. A petrol station and forecourt were built at the roadside.

In October 1966 the Hartford Motors branch opened in the complex dominated by Seacourt Tower, known to some as Botley cathedral.

The Seacourt site was later developed further, with modifications to Hartford's complex and the addition of the Texas and Habitat superstores.

Frank S. Huggins was Deputy Chairman of the Hartwell group in 1964 and was appointed Chairman in 1971. He lived then in Cumnor Rise Road.

The Hartwell Group now comprises a range of companies, including Botley Builders, and premises in several parts of the country. The Group's headquarters are in Seacourt Tower.

Churches

A hundred years ago Anglican members in the Botley area had a choice of churches to attend — at a distance.

People within Cumnor parish looked to St. Michael's in Cumnor.

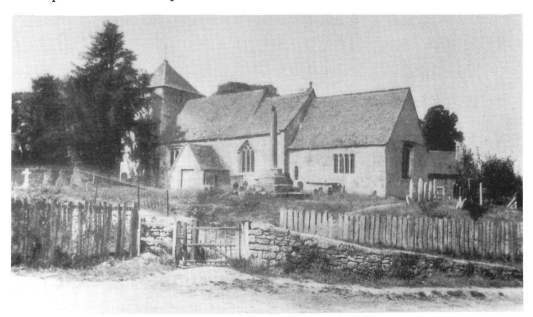

Those in North Hinksey and at Seacourt Farm looked to St. Lawrence's in North Hinksey. This drawing from 1910 shows a gated lane by the side of the church.

The Rev. Osborne-Jones, vicar in 1910, foresaw the growth of Botley, which was soon to be wholly within the parish and sought a site for a second church there. Perhaps he had listened to complaints from Botley families who made the return journey three times every Sunday: to Matins, Sunday School and Evensong. In 1914 he was able to buy a site in Botley. A mission church was erected there, with help from the Diocese.

The mission church in 1955.

By the end of the 1930s it became clear that the small mission church was inadequate for the needs of a rapidly growing population. Thus it is recorded that 'in 1941, on a November night in the war-time black-out, at a meeting presided over by Dr. Gerald Allen, Bishop of Dorchester, the Botley Church Building Fund was opened'. The first contribution was a silver three-penny piece bearing the date 1914, given by a bed-ridden parishioner and, in accordance with a promise made, in September 1957 that same coin was laid under the foundation stone of the new Church of St. Peter and St. Paul in Botley. The church was consecrated in October, 1958.

Schooling

In 1857 a school was built at North Hinksey on glebe land next to the church. An appeal for the building fund spoke of the 'poor and forlorn little village, . . within a mile of Oxford, which cries aloud to the University and to the city for help' The school was provided, according to the rule of the day, 'for the education of children and adults, or children only, of the labouring, manufacturing and other poor classes'. The first lay managers were William Faulkner, gent. (farming on Hinksey Hill); John Weaving, cornfactor; John Hunt, miller (of Botley Mill), and William Button, gent. (farmer at Botley). Here the children of the parish came, at first without compulsion, for an elementary education, though often drawn away by farmers for harvesting and haymaking.

In 1860 a school opened in Cumnor which was available to children in Dean Court, Botley Pound and part of Botley. They had to walk there. This photograph is from about 1930.

North Hinksey School seems to have hit hard times in 1891, for the new vicar, the Revd. Harrison, was thought to be 'unbusinesslike in management'. With three different teachers in charge during the year, the school was found by Inspectors to be 'unsatisfactory'. Harrison was said to be ready to abandon the school in favour of a new Board School, free of church influence, for the Bishop wrote to him: 'I confess I can hardly believe that you are a likely man to be guilty of such treachery towards your people'. In 1894, the school was extended to take 100 pupils.

School group in 1905. The teacher was Mrs Bascombe. Florence Bryant was last pupil but one on the right in the back row.

George King remembered his days there during the Great War: 'I loved our little school, every lesson, every minute'. One lady recalls she hated it. William Woodward, living then at Botley Pound, had cause to remember his first school day in 1913 : 'Set in the roadside bank in Hinksey Lane was a stone. According to legend, if you spat on the stone it brought you luck. I did just that and, on stepping over the stile a little farther on, I found a sixpenny piece. Can you imagine my elation? I had never seen such money!' William Woodward became a Captain on Field Marshal Montgomery's staff in the Second World War. Alice Harvey enjoyed most lessons but not knitting and sewing: 'I always had to knit socks and I hated it. My friend also hated it, especially when we came to the heel, which was the hardest part to do, so we hid them behind the cupboard and said we couldn't find them!'

This photograph was taken in 1927. Known names: Sitting: last but one on right, Dennis Carter; Second row: from left- 2nd Madge Bennett, 3rd Andrew Shorter, 7th Joyce Bennett, 8th Joan Lanchbury. Third row: Maggie Floyd

Some elderly residents remember the school in the 1930s, when Miss Mackenzie (who had differences with the vicar) and later Miss Thatcher ('very strict') was Headmistress, and the infants were in Miss Neale's charge. Even Botley children usually went home for lunch.

After the Great War Botley people began to demand a local school but in 1920 the Abingdon District Council was adamant: 'In view of the present adequate facilities for education at present existing in this District, the Council consider this a distinctly imappropriate moment for the building of a Board school at Botley, having especially in mind the high cost of erection to Berkshire County Council'. At least in 1926 a bus was laid on to Cumnor for children on the Eynsham Road.

In 1938 a new senior school for North Hinksey and Cumnor was built at Botley (senior boys had previously attended St. Frideswide's in Binsey Lane, the girls West Oxford). The headmaster was Mr Harber. This view was taken from where the by-pass bridge now crosses West Way. During the war a girls' school was evacuated to Botley from Kennington, London and Botley School had to work in shifts. Oxford & County Newspapers.

In September 1958 Botley School was reorganised as a primary school — a new secondary school had been built on Arnold's Way and named Matthew Arnold School.

A Botley School photo from 1951, Class J0. Front row: Richard Ray, ?Fay Mitchell, Brian Turner, Jennifer Platt, Colin Hill, — —, ?Jimmy Cooper. Second row: ?Christine Deacon, Robert Boyd, — —, Keith Boyle, Brian Cripps, Colin Thomsett, Peter Edgington, Graham Bunning, Judith Waine. Third row: — —, ?Michael Enever, — —, Norman Howells, Mary Rawlings, — —, — —, David Marriott, — —. Fourth row: ?Kathleen Bull, Ralph Slaney, — —, Colin Weare, — —, John Barnes, Robin Howard, Bobby Freeman, — —. Back row: ?Phillipa Rule, — —, — —, — —, — —, Michael Wesley, Alan Charlet, — —, Victor Bennett. The teacher is Miss Medhurst.

Botley schoolchildren return to school in 1960 after the summer holiday. Oxford & County Newspapers.

A group of Botley schoolchildren cross West Way in September 1968. The elm trees were still standing around Elm Court. The mission church lay beyond the Parade. The crossing patrolman was probably Mr Pratley. Oxford & County Newspapers.

North Hinksey schoolchildren with Miss Cudmore c.1958. Known names: Bottom row (left to right) – 3rd Alistair Day, 7th – Fisher, 8th Brian Coy, 9th – Fisher. Middle row: Pat and Pam Brett, Lorna Bradbury, Miss Cudmore, headmistress, – –, – –, Pamela Bishop. Standing: Adrian Pinnock?, – –, – –, – –, Susan Deadman, Brian Hayward, Pauline Willis, Paul Castle, – –, – –, – –, Roger Alder, – – , Neville Bradbury.

In North Hinksey the increasingly unsatisfactory school buildings were eventually replaced by a new primary school. The plans were first drawn up in 1961 but the school was not completed and opened until September 1974.

This group of children attended Harmsworth Infants School, a private establishment situated on the old Southern By-Pass next to the Scout hut. The photograph was taken in the mid-1950s. Miss Lomax is the teacher and the bespectacled pupil in the centre is Ian Gaisford who succeeded his father in the hairdressing business on Elms Parade.

NORTH HINKSEY AND BOTLEY JUBILEE
CELEBRATIONS

PROGRAMME OF EVENTS

Childrens Jubilee Painting Competition

FRIDAY, 10th JUNE
CHILDRENS JUBILEE CARNIVAL SPORTS
to be held at Botley Primary School
commencing 2 p.m.

SATURDAY, 11th JUNE
16th OXFORD SCOUTS
GRAND JUBILEE FETE
to be held at Botley Primary School
commencing 2 p.m.
Stalls - Sideshows - Penalty Prize - Raffles
FANCY DRESS COMPETITION
Age Groups : 2—5, 6—9 and 10—13 years
(Run by North Hinksey & Botley Jubilee Committee)
SPECIAL GUEST : ROY BURTON (Oxford United)

SATURDAY, 11th JUNE
GRAND JUBILEE DANCE
at ELMS COURT 8 p.m. until 12 midnight
Dancing to the Music of the PUMPKIN PEOPLE
Jubilee Draw will take place during evening.
To be drawn by Roy Burton (Oxford United).
Tickets : £1.50p each including buffet
Tickets available from :
Mrs. Watton, 2 Cedar Road, Botley
Mrs. Bayer, 49 Seacourt Road, Botley

A poster for the 1977 Silver Jubilee celebrations.

The entrance to Matthew Arnold School, built in 1958 as a secondary modern.

Under the headship of the late Joseph Newman (seated centre), Matthew Arnold was successfully reorganised as a comprehensive school. He retired in 1988, having been at the school for 16 years. He died at Exmouth, Devon in 1990. This photograph was taken in 1987.

Two Botley Businesses

Hinkins and Frewin

Hinkins and Frewin, the well-known building firm, developed strong associations with Botley. Herbert Hinkins and Percy Frewin first went into partnership in Oxford, with premises in Walton Well Road. Hinkins had come from Royston in Hertfordshire in 1912 to manage a building firm, J.Simms. Percy Frewin, the son of a carpenter at Chawley Works, went to work at the same firm and a partnership evolved, with the new company becoming 'Limited' in 1926.

In 1927 Hinkins and Frewin needed a larger yard for storing materials and maintaining machinery. It is said that Percy Frewin wanted to buy a large area off Hinksey Lane but couldn't afford it and that Hubert Curtis agreed to share the cost and the land, thus making the two firms neighbours.

A view taken c.1960 shows the yard, behind the properties on West Way.

Hinkins and Frewin gained a well-respected reputation, winning prestigious restoration and building projects at Oxford colleges. They built houses too, particularly in the 1930s, including houses in Raleigh Park Road and Yarnells Road. (More recently they built the new Barclay's Bank and Church Hall on West Way.)

The firm continued to use the Botley yard for plant maintenance. There was a blacksmith on site. In 1974 premises on the main road, adjoining the yard (previously Hartwell's and later Lowe and Oliver) were purchased. Botley then became the company's headquarters.

Arthur H. Hinkins was Chairman and Managing Director for some 12 years before his retirement in 1988. Under him, Hinkins and Frewin continued to play an important part in the restoration of Oxford's fine buildings. The firm has recently been merged and moved to new quarters on the other side of Seacourt Stream.

John Curtis and Sons

John Curtis (1837-1904) came from Wiltshire. In 1860 he married Ellen Barson of Cumnor. By the 1870s he had gained work as a millwright at Botley Mill and rented a cottage at Botley Pound. He had 11 children, William being the eldest son.

An 1893 directory lists John Curtis, engineer, at 'Botley Works' and by 1907 the firm was known as Jn Curtis & Sons, though John, the founder, died in 1904. His sons John, Frank and Ernest took over the business.

This photograph shows some of the family and guests at the wedding of Louisa Curtis c.1909. Left to right: Bottom row: Dorcie, Nellie, Alfred (son of William), Hubert (son of John, Wm's brother), Ruby, Ruth, Nora, Margery, Gladys, Mr Swift 2nd row: Mrs Scoones, Lizzie, John (William's brother), Josie, Carrie, Tilly, William, 'Grandma', Louisa, Robert Smith, Mrs Smith, Lou Smith. 3rd row: Mr Scoones, — —, Alfred Speight, Ernie (brother of William), Ethel, Mrs Moran, Mary Anne, Emma (sister of Ernest), Ann, Edith (daughter of Wm), Herbert (brother of Wm), Daisy Smith, Mrs Jones.

In the early days, Hubert recalled, the firm was 'mostly wheelwrighting and agricultural machinery and repairs. Farm machinery was hired out to local farmers for harvesting, threshing, etc. George King spent some months there: 'There were tractor engines, the forge, the wheelwright's shop, the carpenter's shop, the paint shop, the saw mill. I helped in them all'. These activities were sited at the old timber yard and saw mills until 1927, when Hubert Curtis acquired part of the old gravel pit site off Hinksey Lane. Logs were brought there by the steam traction engine driven by 'Blossom' Trinder, who lived with his mother at the top of Hinksey Lane.

The firm began to extract gravel at Stanton Harcourt, and in 1930 moved to part of Cumnor Meadow at Farmoor (now under the reservoirs). In 1936 Jn Curtis and Sons turned their attention to the extensive gravel terraces at Radley and later moved their offices there. They still retain the Botley site, occupied by tenants.

Changes

Early 1968 seemed to announce 'all change' in Botley. In the foreground the new Baptist Church was taking shape. Further down the road the Elms Court Ballroom was being built. On the left of the picture, work was in progress on the shopping precinct at the rear of Elms Parade. The precinct increased the number of shops at the Parade almost threefold. Photo: Courtesy of J.B.Harris, 8 St Michael's St., Oxford.

Elms Court Ballroom was built in 1968 but by 1984 was proving a very poor investment for the District Council. It was demolished, to make way for Seacourt Hall, while Hartwells erected an adjoining office block. Oxford & County Newspapers.

Botley Pound

Botley Pound began as a small group of cottages on the road to Dean Court and was evidently the site of the pound where stray animals were kept until the owner paid a fine.

Willow Cottage, one of the 18th century cottages. The cottages at Botley Pound were the home of labourers and craftsmen.

The house made of Chawley brick and tiles which was built by Chawley Works. It was, at the turn of the century, served by a narrow gauge railtrack down which tiles were brought for drying in the yard at the rear.

A stone carving set in the wall commemorated Lord Abingdon, lord of Cumnor manor, who owned Chawley Works. Today there is no lord of the manor, and Chawley Brick Works closed down more than 50 years ago.

Dean Court

Dean Court was a medieval hamlet comprising several farms and stood on the 'highway' running west from Botley along the valley to Cumnor Meadow.

This view, taken by Taunt early in the century, looked west along the Eynsham Road from the entrance to Dean Court Farm. The farm buildings on the left are no longer standing.

A sketch of Dean Court Farm in 1980 prior to the development of the site and the building of the Fogwell Road estate to the rear. In 1980 the farm was still being run by William White, having earlier in the century been Nixey's. It was part of the Wytham Estate acquired by the University. Parts of the farmhouse date back to medieval times.

Donald Willis recalled coming to Dean Court Farm with his brother seventy years ago to help with harvesting or go up for a walk in Wytham Woods. 'My brother was well acquainted with Raymong ffennell'. His brother married the famer's daughter.

This house on the south side of Eynsham Road has a long history. For many centuries this was a farmhouse. In 1924 Arthur Wastie was still running the farm there, the out-buildings lying some distance behind it.

A family poses at the back of the house. The Wise family lived there in 1920. The postal address was Botley.

The Dean Court estate was built at the end of the 1950s and in 1960 the local bus service from Oxford was extended here. Dean Court was one of the communities that celebrated the 50th anniversary of D Day, as the photographs below bear witness:

Jason Dallimore leads the sprint to the tape, closely pursued by Terry Kane.

Lined up for the judging of the fancy costume. Sarah holds the tray, with Terry to the right and Uzmar to the left.

Roads

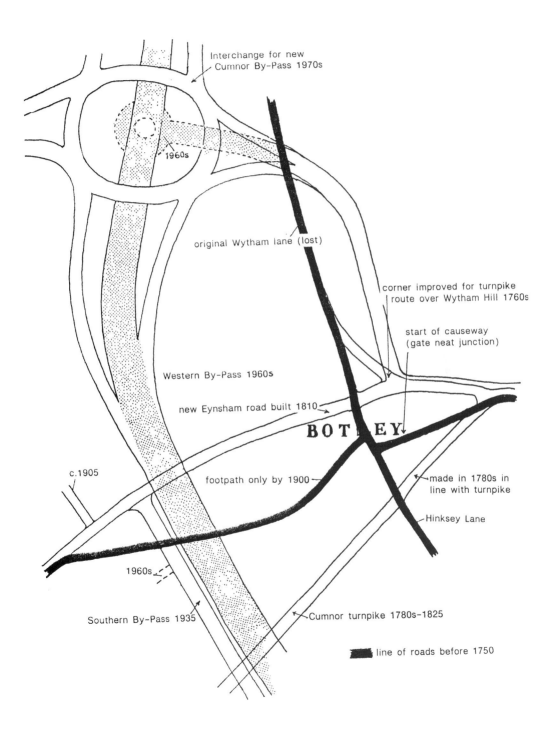

Interchange for new
Cumnor By-Pass 1970s

1960s

original Wytham lane (lost)

corner improved for turnpike
route over Wytham Hill 1760s

start of causeway
(gate neat junction)

Western By-Pass 1960s

new Eynsham road built 1810

BOTLEY

c.1905

footpath only by 1900

made in 1780s in
line with turnpike

Hinksey Lane

1960s

Southern By-Pass 1935

Cumnor turnpike 1780s-1825

line of roads before 1750

The Eynsham Road was the A40 road to Wales until the Northern By-Pass was built in the 1930s and became the main route. In 1936 the Southern By-Pass was built from Hinksey Turn to Botley but ended at what is now West Way, almost opposite Elms Road. The intended continuation of the by-pass north to connect with the new A40 and the Woodstock Road had to wait till 1965, when the existing by-pass was also made a double-carriageway. Botley became an important junction in the regional road network. This position was emphasised with the building of the Cumnor By-Pass (A420) and the huge inter-change at Seacourt. But traffic congestion continues to be a problem. Sharpe's plan in 1947 for a second road into Oxford from Botley is still discussed and recently there have been rumours of the A34 Western By-Pass, now a 'Euroroute' linking the Midlands with Southampton, being widened.

Westminster Way, the original Southern By-Pass.

One effect of the new A420 Cumnor By-Pass was 'infill' development. New estates were allowed on the lands left between the existing built-up boundaries and the new road.

The A34 carves its way across Botley and North Hinksey.

The completion of a pedestrian underpass from Montagu Road under the A34 twenty years later led to complaints that one overdue improvement had created another traffic hazard. In September 1987 residents prepared to greet visitors John Patten M.P. and Peter Bottomley, Transport Minister.

In 1993 enormous traffic disruption was caused by the replacement of the A34 bridge over West Way due to structural failure.

North Hinksey

How different from our modern by-passes was the old lane to the Hinkseys a hundred years ago! The ancient 'green way' was eroded by centuries of wear, so that by 1900 it was several feet below the neighbouring fields — a 'hollow way'. 'It was a very dark, long lane,' Alice Harvey recalled, 'no houses built then. When we had a lot of snow and rain the river would flood over the road'.

Hinksey Lane 100 years ago. 'We knew every turn and twist, every stick and stone', wrote George King. 'On weekdays we ran down the lane to school, carrying a little bag of lunch in bad weather to save doing the journey twice'. Oxfordshire Photographic Archive.

The path from Oxford.

The better-known approach to Hinksey was from Oxford, across the meadows to the ferry. For that reason the village was often called Ferry Hinksey.

The ferry and an alehouse were part of a small estate which in the 15th century was purchased by Brasenose College. The estate farm was sometimes called Library Farm, because the original grant which made the purchase possible had a condition that income from it should be used to buy books for the college library.

The public house called 'The Fishes',by the ferry, shortly before its demolition in 1885. Another has since taken its place.

A view of Hinksey Ferry c.1840.

The ferry crossed to a medieval causeway leading to Ferry Hinksey Road and Osney. This was improved and realigned in the 1880s by Lord Harcourt, the chief landowner in North Hinksey, who built Willow Walk and the bridge over the Seacourt or Hinksey Stream. This scene was photographed just before the ferry closed in 1928.

Hinksey bridge on a lush summer's day. Lord Harcourt built it as part of an access road to a model garden estate for which he had plans drawn in 1880.

NORTH HINKSEY: LORD HARCOURT'S
ESTATE PLAN – 1888

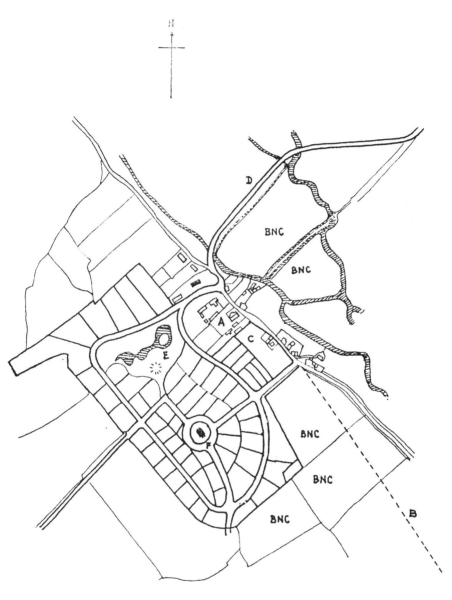

A – Manor Farm
B – Footpath to South Hinksey
C – Set aside for artisans' dwellings
D – New road to Osney
E – Park
F – Conduit
BNC – Brasenose College land

The 1880 plan included a park with a lake, and cottages for artisans. However, the plans came to nought, apart from the bridge and Willow Walk.

Whereas Botley was little-known and largely ignored by travel writers, North Hinksey was known far and wide on account of Matthew Arnold's elegaic poems. Virtually every educated Englishman had heard of Hinksey.

In 1872 the village became a focus of national interest when John Ruskin undertook a social experiment to show his gentlemen scholars at Oxford the virtues of physical labour. With Lord Harcourt's permission he engaged his students in building a better road along the village green. The value of physical labour had evidently not been appreciated by the local inhabitants, who had allowed their lane to fall into such a wretched condition that they had difficulty in going to their farmwork.

Among the students involved who later became well-known was Oscar Wilde. Ruskin's project was ridiculed in the national press and was not a marked success. It was ahead of its time.

The village green changed little during the 19th century, for all Arnold's nostalgic complaint.

The village street leading to the 'green' today.

Three views of 'Ruskin's Cottage', where the road-building and improvements started.

1900.

1920.

1995.

Village life

Village life was still quiet in the early period between the wars. 'There were no lights in the village and we had to have oil lamps or candles', Alice Harvey recalled. 'Harvest and haymaking were busy times and the children loved to ride back from the fields on the carts loaded with warm, sweet-smelling hay'.

The Conduit House, photographed by Taunt 90 years ago. It was built by Otto Nicholson in 1616 but the same source had supplied Osney Abbey in medieval times. In the 1920s it still provided the village water supply and though the Manor Farm could boast, according to the selling agents in 1926, 'an inexhaustable supply', the cottages all depended on two taps (one in the lane, the other on the green), which were unreliable in summer.

Vandalism is not a modern phenomenon. Who carved this so long ago into the stone of the conduit house ? An Oxford student ? A member of the local Faulkner family?

Changes in North Hinksey

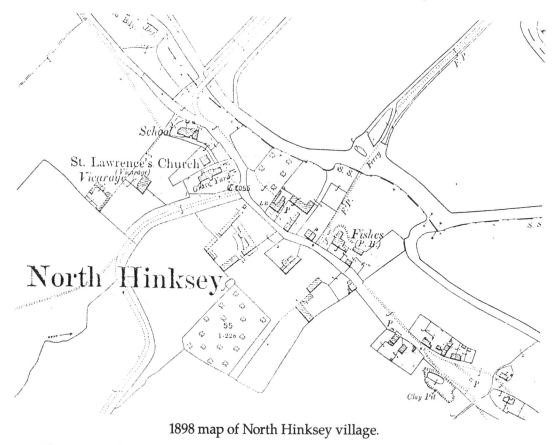

1898 map of North Hinksey village.

The centre of Lord Harcourt's estate (the Harcourts actually resided at Nuneham Courtney and Stanton Harcourt) was Hinksey Manor Farm, which included the medieval Monks' Barn.

Monks' Barn, photographed by Taunt at the beginning of the century. It has since fallen into ruin but can still be seen.

In 1926 Lord Harcourt decided, as Lord Abingdon had already done, to dispose of his estates which the farming recession had made unprofitable.

By direction of the Trustees of the Rt. Hon. VISCOUNT HARCOURT.

O X F O R D

On the Berkshire side of the River, within three-quarters of a mile of Oxford Station.

THAT DELIGHTFUL

OLD STONE-BUILT RESIDENCE

known as the

MANOR FARM HOUSE,

FERRY HINKSEY.

In an old-world rural setting, fronted by an old walled-in Garden, and containing 9 Bedrooms, 2 or 3 Reception Rooms and Ample Offices.

EXCELLENT & COMMODIOUS BUILDINGS

and LAND, in all about

3¼ ACRES,

presenting unusual opportunities for restoration, also

ELEVEN PICTURESQUE OLD COTTAGES

Stone-built with Thatched Roofs, comprising the greater part of the Village of Ferry Hinksey.

WHICH MESSRS.

NICHOLAS

LONDON AND READING.

Will (unless acceptable offers be made privately beforehand), offer by Auction IN LOTS, at

THE CLARENDON HOTEL, OXFORD,

On Wednesday, 21st July, 1926,

At 2.30 p.m. precisely.

Particulars, Plan and Conditions of Sale may be had of the Solicitors, Messrs. WALKER, MARTINEAU & Co., 36, Theobald's Road, W.C.1 ; Mr. HARRY GALE, The Estate Office, Nuneham Courtnay, Oxford ; or of the Auctioneers, Messrs. NICHOLAS,

4, Albany Court Yard, Piccadilly, W.1,

And at Station Road, Reading, Berks.

Most of the village cottages were sold at the same auction. The cottagers were: Lot 1 (Ruskin's Cottage on SE corner) Lady Raleigh, 2 Mr Peart and Mr Sawyer (at 4s rent a week), 3 Mrs Launchbury, 4 Walter Floyd, 5 Mr Greening, 6 Walter Bishop and Mr W. Greening, 7 Mr J. Howard, 8 Mr W. Greening. Greening was farming and had leased cottages for his men.

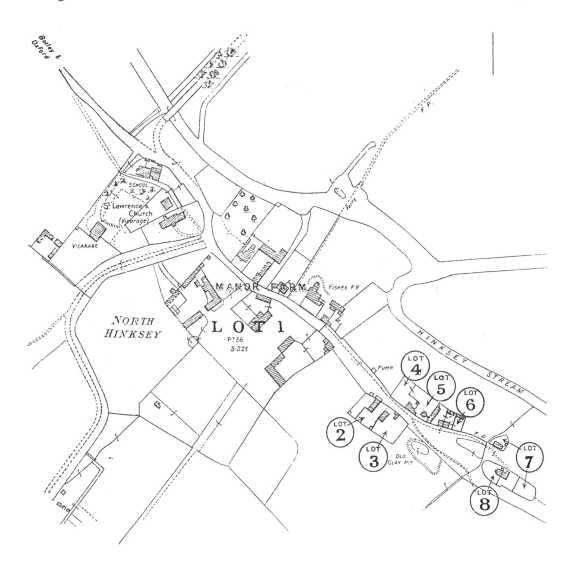

When the manor house came up for sale in 1969, it was, as the agents say, 'in need of improvement'. Oxford & County Newspapers.

A view of the property today from the south.

The manor farm was sold in 1926 without its lands, because Lord Harcourt had revived the idea of a model estate development on the slopes of Hinksey Hill. This was more extensive than the 1880 plan. The two parts of the huge estate were to be separated by a golf course, an idea which became reality in 1995, and a feature was retained around the Conduit House (built in 1616 by Otto Nicholson, who tapped the hillside springs to provide a piped water supply to central Oxford). The park feature was omitted because Raymond ffennel of Wytham had just bought land above the church and given it to Oxford for a park, to be known as Raleigh Park. Lord Harcourt's scheme included shops and a social club on the site now occupied by Westminster College.

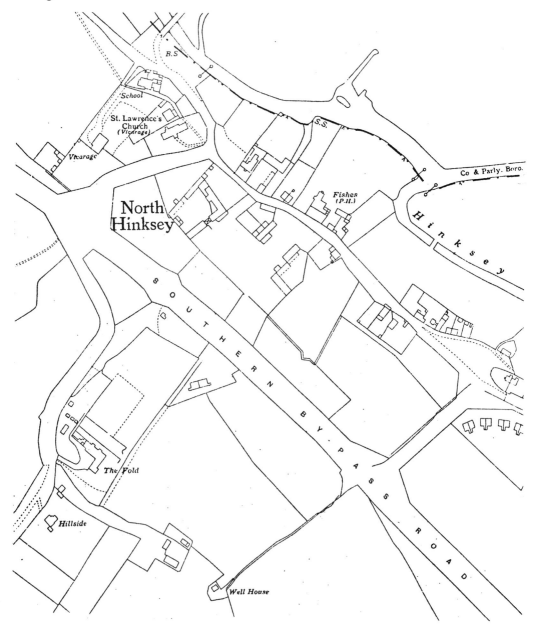

Again the ambitious project did not go ahead, though a few houses were built off Harcourt Hill lane. One reason may have been the expressed concern of the Oxford Trust and others over Oxford's suburban growth. A regional survey in 1930 observed that Hinksey's slopes were likely to be developed rapidly as a residential area, a matter to be regretted, but 'North Hinksey, which is at present quite unspoiled, should be, as it were, roped around and protected from any further building in its immediate proximity'.

North or Ferry Hinksey.

PRIVATE RESIDENTS.

Beaumont Miss W. M. School ho
Blunsdon Ernest Rd. Lilliers, Hinksey la
Parker Walt. Arcadia, Hinksey la
Robinson Rev. Edwd. Shinn B.A. The Vicarage
Tilby William Francis
Tomkinson William Shirley, Bungalow
Toynbee Miss Winifred, The Fold
Wigg Charles Hector, Hillside

COMMERCIAL.

Burrows Ivy May (Mrs.), genl. shop
Greening W. (Mrs), farmer, Hinksey hill
Hedges William, farmer, College farm
Morris Arthur, The Fishes inn

Kelly's Directory for 1930.

NORTH HINKSEY: DEVELOPMENT PLAN 1924
for Lord Harcourt

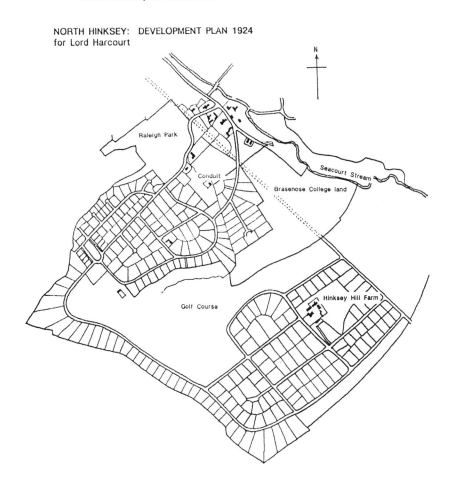

Map of North Hinksey in 1937.

St. Lawrence's Church

The centre of North Hinksey village was the medieval church of St. Lawrence, once a chapel of ease to Cumnor but a parish church in its own right from around 1725.

Taunt's photograph of the church in 1904.

Sketch made in 1909 for Brabant's 'Berkshire', shortly before the church restoration.

In 1910 the vicar, the Rev. Osborne-Jones, successfully raised funds for the necessary restoration of the building, particularly the roof.

Repairs in progress in 1910.

One resident remembered well the Sunday School outings in the 1920s. 'We always went to Beacon Hill, which is just this side of the Toll Gate at Eynsham. Two wagons drawn by carthorses would carry about 20 of us and we all had to take our own cups or mugs. We stopped on the way at a farmhouse where the farmer's wife provided us with a nice tea in a field near the house. After tea we traipsed up to Beacon Hill to have races and the winners were given sweets'.

St. Lawrence's parish church in 1960. Today the church stands close to a new Diocesan Centre and to the thrumming traffic of the A34. The peace was first disturbed in 1935 when the Southern By-Pass went through the glebe lands.

North Hinksey School

A second important focus of village life was, of course, the school.

This photograph was taken outside the parish church on the occasion of the old school's centenary in 1957. The school's early history has already been mentioned.

In 1961 plans were first drawn for a new primary school as the old school was increasingly unsuited to the needs of modern education. It was not until September 1974 however that the new school was built and opened.

North Hinksey children, and no doubt their parents, enjoying a 'Victorian Evening' at the end of the Christmas Term, c.1983.

Enjoying the environment of the new primary school.

Maurice Tubb, photographed here at the front of the premises, was Head Teacher at North Hinksey for 17 years. He retired in 1995.

In 1959 new buildings appeared on the hill above Hinksey, but not those once conceived by Lord Harcourt. A large site at the top of Harcourt Hill was purchased for the Westminster Methodist Teacher Training College, which moved out of London. The college chapel and buildings are now a familiar feature on the Hinksey skyline, though they were criticised by Pevsner for the 'mildly blocky neo-Georgian style'. The college now offers a wide range of courses and facilities.

The Rapid Growth

In 1931 the census still showed only 53 dwellings in North Hinksey parish, including Botley. By 1991 there were 1,705, of which 80% were owner-occupied.

Few parts of Britain experienced such a rapid explosion of housing and population as occurred here between 1930 and 1960, welding the old hamlets of Botley and North Hinksey together in one arm of Oxford's suburban expansion.

In 1931 hardly anyone owned a car and few houses were built with a garage. In 1991 75% of households owned at least one car (a quarter possessed two cars).

Sketch map.

A hundred years ago a third of those employed were working on farms, a fifth in labouring jobs, a quarter in trade. In 1991 only one employed person in a hundred was working in agriculture; almost a quarter were engaged in manufacturing or technical jobs, and as many in distribution and catering.

At the beginning of the century a majority of the working people in Botley and North Hinksey were employed locally. Today, although many more jobs have been created here, a majority of working people commute to the city or elsewhere. The increasing problems in central Oxford have however led some firms to relocate in Botley.

A hundred years ago 42% of the parish population were aged under 15, and 8% were over 65. In 1991 15.2% of the population were under 15 years of age, and the percentage of those over 65 was 20.4%. Botley, with North Hinksey parish, thus shares with the nation as a whole a more affluent but ageing population.

The centre of Old Botley amid the new.